INTRODUCTION

In the intricate tapestry of life, every day we live we encounter various experiences and emotions that shape our journey. Among these, there is depression which casts a heavy burden, affecting individuals in profound and often invisible ways. It clouds the mind, dampens the spirit, and drains the colors from even the brightest moments. Yet, it is essential to remember that depression does not define who we are, nor does it hold the power to dictate our future.

This book, "Life's Journey: A Guide to Steering Clear of Depression," is an empowering resource meticulously crafted to help you reclaim your life from the clutches of depression. Within its pages, you will discover insights, strategies, and compassionate guidance to guide you towards resilience, self-empowerment, and the pursuit of a life free from the grips of depression.

Chapter by chapter, we will explore the multifaceted nature of depression, unraveling its steps and shedding light on its causes and effects. We will delve into the importance of building a strong support system, nurturing meaningful connections, and seeking professional assistance when needed and other factors. Together, we will delve into the depths of emotional resilience, uncovering tools to cope with adversity and bounce back stronger than ever before. We will uncover the transformative power of self-care, unravel the secrets of managing stress, and embrace the art of setting realistic goals that align with our true passions and values.

As we embark on this transformative journey, we will navigate through the labyrinth of negative thinking, replacing self-doubt with self-compassion and rekindling our innate sense of worth. We will explore the practice of mindfulness, allowing us to fully embrace the present moment, cultivate inner peace, and awaken our senses to the beauty that surrounds us. And throughout it all, we will challenge the stigma surrounding mental health, opening up avenues for understanding, acceptance, and healing.

While this book serves as a valuable guide, it is important to acknowledge that it does not substitute professional medical advice. If you are currently experiencing depression or suspect that you may be, I strongly encourage you to seek the expertise of a qualified mental health professional who can provide tailored support and guidance to address your unique needs.

Remember, dear reader, that you are not alone on this transformative journey. Within these pages, you will find solace, hope, and practical tools to guide you towards a life that is abundant with joy, purpose, and emotional well-being.

Together, let us embark on this path of healing, resilience, and self-discovery, as we navigate life's challenges, steer clear of depression, and embrace the boundless possibilities that await us.

Chapter 1: UNDERSTANDING DEPRESSION

1.1 Defining Depression: A Multifaceted Mental Health Condition

Depression is a multifaceted mental health condition that affects millions of people worldwide. It is characterized by persistent feelings of sadness, hopelessness, and a loss of interest or pleasure in activities that were once enjoyable. Depression goes beyond the normal ups and downs of life, lasting for an extended period and interfering with daily functioning. It is essential to understand that depression is not a sign of weakness or a character flaw but a legitimate medical condition that requires attention and support.

Depression can manifest in various forms, such as major depressive disorder, persistent depressive disorder (dysthymia), postpartum depression, seasonal affective disorder, and others. Each form has its unique features and may require specific interventions or treatments. By recognizing and acknowledging the presence of depression, individuals can take proactive steps towards seeking help and reclaiming their mental well-being.

1.2 Recognizing the Signs and Symptoms: Navigating the Emotional Landscape

Recognizing the signs and symptoms of depression is crucial for early intervention and support. While the experience of depression can vary from person to person, common indicators include:

1. Persistent feelings of sadness, emptiness, or despair
2. Loss of interest or pleasure in previously enjoyed activities
3. Significant changes in appetite and weight
4. Sleep disturbances, such as insomnia or oversleeping
5. Fatigue, lack of energy, or diminished motivation
6. Difficulty concentrating, making decisions, or remembering things
7. Feelings of guilt, worthlessness, or excessive self-criticism
8. Physical symptoms like headaches, digestive issues, or chronic pain
9. Social withdrawal and isolation
10. Recent thoughts of death or suicide

It is important to note that experiencing a few of these symptoms does not automatically indicate depression. However, if these symptoms persist for more than two weeks and significantly impact daily life, it is crucial to seek professional evaluation and support.

1.3 Exploring the Causes and Triggers: Unraveling the Complexity

Depression is a complex condition influenced by a combination of genetic, biological, environmental, and psychological factors. Some potential causes and triggers of depression include:

- ❖ Biological Factors: Imbalances in brain chemicals (neurotransmitters) like serotonin and norepinephrine can contribute to depression. Genetic predisposition may also play a role, as individuals with a family history of depression may be more susceptible.

- ❖ Environmental Factors: Life experiences, such as trauma, abuse, neglect, or significant losses, can increase the risk of depression. Chronic stress, financial difficulties, or living in an unsupportive or abusive environment can also contribute to its development.

- ❖ Co-occurring Conditions: Depression often coexists with other mental health disorders, such as anxiety, substance abuse, or eating disorders. These conditions can interact and exacerbate each other's symptoms, making effective treatment more challenging.

- ❖ Hormonal Changes: Hormonal fluctuations, such as those occurring during puberty, pregnancy, or menopause, can contribute to depressive episodes. Postpartum hormonal changes can trigger postpartum depression in some individuals.

- ❖ Personality Traits: Certain personality traits, such as low self-esteem, a pessimistic outlook, or a history of perfectionism, can increase vulnerability to depression.

By delving into the depths of depression and gaining a comprehensive understanding of its nature, signs, symptoms, causes, and triggers, individuals can embark on a journey of healing and resilience.

Chapter 2: BUILDING A SUPPORT SYSTEM

2.1 The Importance of Social Connections: Embracing the Power of Relationships

In the journey to steer clear of depression, building and maintaining a strong support system is paramount. Social connections provide a sense of belonging, understanding, and emotional support that can be invaluable during challenging times. Research consistently shows that individuals with robust social networks have better mental health outcomes and a reduced risk of depression.

Social connections come in various forms, including relationships with family, friends, romantic partners, colleagues, and community members. Each of these relationships plays a unique role in providing different types of support. Family relationships can offer unconditional love and support, while friendships provide companionship, empathy, and shared experiences. Romantic relationships offer intimacy, emotional support, and a deep sense of connection.

Building a supportive network of relationships is crucial for maintaining emotional well-being and preventing depression. Humans are social beings, and having a strong support system can provide comfort, guidance, and a sense of belonging.

2.2 Nurturing Relationships: Quality Over Quantity

While the quantity of relationships is important, it is the quality of those connections that truly matters. Building meaningful relationships involves investing time, effort, and emotional energy into cultivating connections that are mutually beneficial and supportive. It is about surrounding yourself with people who uplift, inspire, and genuinely care about your well-being.

Nurturing relationships requires open and honest communication. Sharing your thoughts, emotions, and experiences with trusted individuals allows them to better understand your journey and offer appropriate support. Encourage reciprocity in your relationships, creating a space where both parties can share and be heard.

Remember, not all relationships will be equally supportive or positive. It is essential to evaluate the impact of your relationships on your well-being. If certain relationships consistently bring you down or contribute to your depressive symptoms, it may be necessary to reassess their place in your life and set boundaries to protect your mental health and peace of mind.

2.3 Seeking Professional Help: The Power of Therapeutic Support

While the support of loved ones is invaluable, professional help is a vital component in managing and overcoming depression. Mental health professionals possess specialized knowledge and expertise in addressing mental health conditions. They can provide guidance, support, and evidence-based treatments tailored to your unique needs.

Therapy, such as cognitive-behavioral therapy (CBT), can help identify and challenge negative thought patterns, develop healthy coping mechanisms, and build resilience. Other therapeutic approaches, such as interpersonal therapy (IPT), focus on improving relationships and communication skills. In some cases, medication may be prescribed to alleviate depressive symptoms.

Seeking professional help requires courage and a willingness to prioritize your well-being. Remember that reaching out for support is not a sign of weakness but a proactive step towards healing and growth. Mental health professionals are trained to provide a safe, non-judgmental space where you can explore your emotions, gain insights into your thought patterns, and develop effective strategies to manage and overcome depression so try your best as hard as it may be to open up to them and let them know what you're going through even if its little by little try to speak out.

2.4 Support from Friends and Family: Strengthening Bonds

Friends and family members can play a crucial role in supporting you on your journey to steer clear of depression. Communicating openly and honestly with your loved ones about your experiences can foster understanding and empathy. Encourage them to educate themselves about depression, helping them gain insight into the condition and how they can best support you.

While friends and family may not have professional expertise, their emotional support and presence can be immensely comforting. Engage in activities together that promote well-being, such as going for walks, sharing meals, or pursuing shared hobbies. Engaging in these positive experiences can strengthen the bond and create meaningful connections.

However, it is important to remember that not everyone may fully understand or know how to provide the support you need. Be patient and communicate your needs clearly, expressing what helps and what may be triggering or unhelpful. Setting boundaries is essential to protect your well-being and ensure that your relationships remain healthy and supportive.

Additionally, consider exploring support groups or online communities where you can connect with individuals who have experienced or are currently experiencing similar struggles with depression. These communities provide a sense of belonging and empathy, allowing you to share experiences, exchange insights, and receive support from those who truly understand.

Support goups can take various forms, including in-person meetings, online forums, or virtual support communities. They offer a safe space where you can express yourself openly, discuss challenges, and learn from the experiences of others. By participating in support groups, you can gain a sense of validation, reduce feelings of isolation, and gather valuable strategies for managing and overcoming depression.

When engaging with support groups or online communities, it is important to exercise caution and ensure that the environment is supportive, respectful, and moderated by trained professionals or experienced individuals. Seek out communities that align with your values and provide a sense of safety and authenticity.

2.5   Being a Supportive Friend

Building a supportive network is a two-way street. It is equally important to offer support and be there for others as it is to receive support. Consider the following practices:

- Practice active listening: Be fully present and attentive when someone is sharing their thoughts and feelings with you. Listen without judgment and offer empathy and understanding.

- Validate their experiences: Acknowledge and validate the emotions and experiences of your friends and loved ones. Let them know that their feelings are valid and that you are there to support them.

- Offer assistance: Be proactive in offering your help and assistance when needed. Whether it's providing practical support or simply being there to lend an ear, let your loved ones know that you are available and willing to help.

- Check-in regularly: Take the initiative to check in on your friends and loved ones regularly. Show genuine interest in their well-being and make an effort to maintain the connection. Small gestures of reaching out can make a big difference in someone's life.
- Practice empathy and compassion: Put yourself in the shoes of others and try to understand their perspectives and experiences. Offer compassion and support without judgment.

2.6 Cultivating Self-Support: The Importance of Self-Care

In addition to external support, nurturing your own well-being through self-care is vital for steering clear of depression. Self-care involves intentionally prioritizing activities and practices that promote physical, emotional, and mental well-being. It is about recognizing your own needs, setting boundaries, and engaging in activities that bring you joy, relaxation, and fulfillment.

Self-care practices can vary widely depending on individual preferences, but some examples include:

- Engaging in regular exercise and physical activity to boost mood and reduce stress.

- Practicing mindfulness and meditation to cultivate present-moment awareness and reduce rumination.

- Getting adequate sleep to support overall mental and physical health.

- Nourishing your body with a balanced diet that includes nutrient-rich foods.

- Engaging in hobbies, creative pursuits, or activities that bring you a sense of fulfillment.

- Prioritizing relaxation and stress reduction techniques, such as deep breathing exercises or taking soothing baths.

- Setting realistic goals and celebrating small achievements along the way.

- Engaging in activities that promote social connection and positive relationships.

Remember, self-care is not selfish but a necessary investment in your own well-being. By taking care of yourself, you strengthen your resilience and ability to navigate life's challenges, including depression.

NOTE: Building a support system is an essential component in steering clear of depression. Surrounding yourself with caring individuals who offer understanding, empathy, and support can provide a lifeline during difficult times. Seek professional help when needed and consider joining support groups or online communities for additional support from those who share similar experiences. Prioritize self-care to nurture your own well-being and resilience. By cultivating a strong support system and engaging in self-support practices, you empower yourself to navigate the challenges of depression and embrace a life of emotional well-being and fulfillment.

Chapter 3: DEVELOPING EMOTIONAL RESILIENCE AND MINDSET

3.1 Understanding Emotional Resilience

Emotional resilience is the ability to adapt, cope, and bounce back from adversity, including the challenges that depression may bring. It involves cultivating inner strength, emotional well-being, and a positive mindset to navigate life's ups and downs. Developing emotional resilience is a valuable skill that can help you steer clear of depression and maintain a sense of balance and stability.

3.2 Cultivating Emotional Awareness

Emotional awareness is the foundation of emotional resilience. It involves recognizing, understanding, and accepting your own emotions without judgment. By becoming more aware of your emotions, you can effectively manage and regulate them, preventing them from overwhelming you and leading to depressive episodes.

Practice mindfulness techniques to cultivate present-moment awareness of your emotions. Pay attention to the physical sensations associated with different emotions and try to identify and label them. Regularly check in with yourself to gauge your emotional state and make adjustments as needed.

Remember, all emotions are valid, and it is essential to allow yourself to experience them fully. Avoid suppressing or ignoring your emotions, as this can contribute to increased stress and the risk of developing depression. Instead, create a safe space for yourself to express and process your emotions, whether through journaling, talking to a trusted friend, or engaging in creative outlets.

3.3 **Building Coping Mechanisms**

Coping mechanisms are strategies and techniques that help you manage stress, navigate challenging situations, and maintain emotional well-being. Developing a toolbox of healthy coping mechanisms is essential in building emotional resilience and avoiding the downward spiral of depression.

Identify coping mechanisms that work best for you. These can include:

- Seeking support: Reach out to your support system, whether it's family, friends, or a therapist. Expressing your feelings and seeking guidance can provide valuable emotional support.

- Engaging in hobbies and creative outlets: Find activities that bring you joy and allow you to express yourself, such as painting, playing an instrument, writing, or gardening.

- Practicing self-compassion: Treat yourself with kindness, understanding, and self-acceptance. Be gentle with yourself during challenging times and practice self-care without judgment.

- Utilizing cognitive reframing: Challenge negative thoughts and replace them with more realistic and positive perspectives. This can help shift your mindset and reduce depressive thinking patterns.

- Setting boundaries: Establish clear boundaries in your relationships and commitments to protect your mental and emotional well-being. Learn to say no when necessary and prioritize your needs.

3.4   **Developing a Growth Mindset**

A growth mindset is the belief that our abilities and intelligence can be developed through effort, learning, and perseverance. Adopting a growth mindset can empower you to overcome obstacles and view challenges as opportunities for growth. Consider the following strategies:

- Embrace a learning attitude: Approach challenges and setbacks as learning experiences. Instead of seeing them as failures, focus on the lessons they provide and the potential for personal growth.

- Cultivate optimism: Foster a positive outlook on life and believe in your ability to overcome difficulties. Practice reframing negative thoughts into positive ones and seek the silver lining in challenging situations.

3.5   **Developing a Positive Mindset**

Fostering a positive mindset is crucial in cultivating emotional resilience. While it may not eliminate all negative experiences, a positive outlook can help you navigate challenges with greater ease and bounce back from setbacks.

Practice gratitude by regularly acknowledging and appreciating the positive aspects of your life. Keep a gratitude journal or take a few moments each day to reflect on the things you are thankful for. This practice can help shift your focus from negative aspects to positive ones.

Engage in positive self-talk by challenging self-critical and negative thoughts. Replace them with affirming and encouraging statements. Treat yourself with kindness, compassion, and understanding.

Surround yourself with positive influences, such as uplifting books, inspiring podcasts, or supportive and optimistic individuals. Seek out activities and experiences that bring you joy, laughter, and a sense of fulfillment.

Remember that developing a positive mindset takes time and practice. Be patient with yourself and allow room for growth and learning.

Incorporating these strategies into your life can help you develop emotional resilience, enabling you to navigate the challenges of depression and steer clear of its grip. Here are some additional aspects to consider in developing emotional resilience:

3.5 Building Problem-Solving Skills

Developing effective problem-solving skills is crucial in managing stress and preventing the escalation of depressive symptoms. When faced with challenges, having the ability to identify potential solutions, evaluate their effectiveness, and take action can significantly impact your well-being.

Start by breaking down problems into smaller, manageable parts. This allows you to approach them with a clearer perspective. Brainstorm potential solutions and consider the pros and cons of each. Seek advice from trusted individuals or professionals who can offer guidance and support.

Remember that problem-solving is an ongoing process. It may require trial and error, and not every solution will yield immediate results. Embrace a growth mindset that acknowledges the value of learning from mistakes and setbacks. Celebrate your successes, no matter how small, as they contribute to your overall progress.

3.6 Cultivating Optimism and Resilient Thinking

Optimism and resilient thinking play a vital role in developing emotional resilience. Optimism involves maintaining a positive outlook and expecting favorable outcomes, even in the face of adversity. Resilient thinking involves reframing negative experiences and setbacks in a way that promotes growth and learning.

Practice reframing negative situations by looking for potential opportunities or lessons learned. Shift your focus from what went wrong to what you can do differently moving forward. Embrace challenges as opportunities for personal growth and resilience-building.

Surround yourself with positive and supportive individuals who embody optimism and resilience. Their influence can have a profound impact on your mindset and outlook. Engage in conversations that foster positivity, hope, and encouragement.

Engage in activities that promote optimism and self-belief, such as affirmations, visualization exercises, or creating a vision board that reflects your goals and aspirations. These practices can help reinforce a positive mindset and build confidence in your ability to overcome obstacles.

3.7 Embracing Self-Reflection and Learning

Self-reflection is a powerful tool for personal growth and emotional resilience. Set aside dedicated time to reflect on your experiences, emotions, and thought patterns. This practice allows you to gain insights into yourself, understand your triggers, and identify patterns that may contribute to depressive episodes.

Journaling can be a helpful tool for self-reflection. Write about your thoughts, emotions, and experiences, allowing yourself to explore and process them. Consider seeking professional guidance, such as therapy, to gain deeper insights into your inner world and develop strategies for personal growth.

Be open to learning from your experiences. Embrace a mindset of curiosity and self-discovery. Treat each day as an opportunity for growth and learning. Embrace new challenges and step out of your comfort zone. Embrace failures as valuable lessons and celebrate successes as milestones on your journey.

By developing emotional resilience, cultivating a positive mindset, and honing problem-solving skills, you can enhance your ability to steer clear of depression and effectively navigate life's challenges. Remember that building emotional resilience is an ongoing process that requires patience, self-compassion, and a commitment to personal growth. Embrace the journey and empower yourself to live a life of emotional well-being and fulfillment.

NOTE: Cultivating resilience and developing a positive mindset are crucial for steering clear of depression and maintaining emotional well-being. By adopting a growth mindset, practicing self-care, developing problem-solving skills, fostering positive thinking, cultivating emotional intelligence, and embracing resilience in the face of setbacks, you can build inner strength and navigate life's challenges with greater ease. Remember that resilience is a skill that can be nurtured and developed over time. With commitment and practice, you can enhance your resilience and lead a more fulfilling and balanced life.

Chapter 4: LIFESTYLE FACTORS FOR EMOTIONAL WELL-BEING

4.1   The Impact of Lifestyle on Mental Health

The way we live our lives and the choices we make on a daily basis can significantly impact our emotional well-being. In this chapter, we will explore lifestyle factors that can help steer clear of depression and promote a healthier mental state.

4.2   Prioritizing Physical Health

Physical health and mental health are interconnected. Taking care of your body plays a crucial role in maintaining emotional well-being and preventing depression. Here are some key aspects to consider:

- Engage in regular exercise: Physical activity releases endorphins, which are natural mood-boosting chemicals. Aim for at least 30 minutes of moderate exercise most days of the week. Find activities you enjoy, such as walking, dancing, swimming, or practicing yoga or anything that helps yoy sweat and move your body.

- Maintain a balanced diet: Nourish your body with a variety of nutritious foods. Include plenty of fruits, vegetables, whole grains, lean proteins, and healthy fats in your diet. Avoid excessive consumption of processed foods, sugary snacks, and caffeinated beverages, as they can negatively impact your mood and energy levels.

- Get sufficient sleep: Lack of sleep can contribute to mood disturbances and increase the risk of depression. Aim for 7-9 hours of quality sleep each night. Establish a consistent sleep schedule, create a relaxing bedtime routine, and ensure your sleep environment is comfortable and conducive to rest.

4.3　**Stress Management Techniques**

Chronic stress can take a toll on your mental health and increase the risk of depression. Developing effective stress management techniques is essential for maintaining emotional well-being. Consider incorporating the following practices into your life:

- Time management: Prioritize tasks, set realistic goals, and break them down into manageable steps. Avoid overloading yourself with excessive responsibilities and create a healthy work-life balance.

- Engage in hobbies and enjoyable activities: Dedicate time to activities that bring you joy and help you relax. This can include reading, listening to music, spending time in nature, practicing mindfulness, or engaging in creative pursuits.

- Foster healthy boundaries: Learn to say no when necessary and set boundaries to protect your time, energy, and well-being. Avoid overcommitting yourself and allocate time for self-care and relaxation.

4.4　**Mindful Technology Use**

While technology can offer many benefits, excessive and unhealthy use of technology can contribute to stress and negatively impact mental health. Consider the following strategies for mindful technology use:

- Set Time for Tech usage: Establish specific timeframes for technology use, such as designating tech-free hours before bed or during meals. Create tech-free zones in your home, such as your bedroom, to promote relaxation and better sleep.

- Have Resting Hours / Breaks: Take regular breaks from technology, whether it's for a few hours, a day, or even a weekend. Use this time to engage in offline activities, connect with loved ones, or pursue hobbies.

- Filter your digital environment: Curate your online experiences by unfollowing or muting accounts that induce negative emotions or comparison. Surround yourself with positive and uplifting content that inspires and motivates you.

4.5 **Cultivating Meaningful Connections and Activities**

Nurturing meaningful connections and engaging in activities that align with your values can contribute to a sense of purpose, fulfillment, and emotional well-being. Consider the following:

- Foster supportive relationships: Surround yourself with positive and supportive individuals who uplift and inspire you. Cultivate deep and meaningful connections based on mutual respect and understanding.

- Engage in meaningful activities: Find activities that bring a sense of purpose and fulfillment to your life. This can include volunteering, pursuing hobbies, engaging in creative outlets, or contributing to causes that resonate with you. Engaging in activities that align with your values can provide a sense of meaning and fulfillment, which can help steer clear of depression.

- Practice active listening: Deepen your connections with others by actively listening and showing genuine interest in their experiences and perspectives. This fosters empathy, understanding, and stronger relationships.

- Seek social support: Reach out to your support system when you need help or simply want to share your thoughts and feelings. Open up about your experiences with trusted friends, family members, or support groups. Remember that seeking support is a sign of strength, not weakness.

4.6 **Cultivating a Healthy Work-Life Balance**

Finding a healthy balance between work and personal life is essential for maintaining emotional well-being and avoiding burnout. Consider the following strategies:

- Set boundaries: Establish clear boundaries between your work and personal life. Define specific times when you are fully present and available for personal activities and relationships. Avoid overworking or bringing work-related stress into your personal time.

- Take regular breaks: Incorporate short breaks throughout your workday to relax and recharge. Use this time to engage in activities that bring you joy and help alleviate stress.

- Prioritize self-care: Make self-care a non-negotiable part of your routine. Dedicate time to activities that promote relaxation, self-reflection, and personal growth. This can include exercise, meditation, hobbies, or simply spending quality time with loved ones.

- Seek support at work: If work-related stress is a significant contributor to your mental health challenges, consider seeking support within your workplace. Talk to a supervisor, human resources, or a trusted colleague who can provide guidance or resources.

4.7 **Creating an Environment Conducive to Well-being**

Your physical environment can impact your mental well-being. Consider the following tips for creating an environment that supports emotional well-being:

- Declutter and organize your space: A clean and organized environment can promote a sense of calm and reduce feelings of overwhelm. Take time to declutter your living and working spaces, creating a more peaceful and harmonious atmosphere.

- Incorporate elements of nature: Bring nature indoors by adding plants, flowers, or natural elements to your environment. Exposure to nature has been shown to reduce stress and improve mood.

- Design a calming space: Create a designated area in your home where you can relax, unwind, and engage in activities that promote well-being. This can be a cozy corner for reading, a meditation space, or a calming room filled with soothing scents and soft lighting.

NOTE: By prioritizing physical health, managing stress, practicing mindful technology use, nurturing connections, cultivating a healthy work-life balance, and creating an environment conducive to well-being, you can greatly enhance your emotional well-being and steer clear of depression. Remember that lifestyle changes take time and consistency, so be patient and compassionate with yourself as you incorporate these practices into your life.

Chapter 5: Self-Care and Self-Compassion for Emotional Well-being

5.1   The Importance of Self-Care

Self-care is a fundamental practice for maintaining emotional well-being and preventing depression. It involves actively nurturing and prioritizing your physical, emotional, and mental health. In this chapter, we will explore different aspects of self-care and how they contribute to a balanced and fulfilling life.

5.2   Physical Self-Care

Physical self-care involves taking care of your body's needs and promoting physical well-being. Here are some key areas to consider:

> ➢ Prioritize sleep: Aim for a consistent sleep schedule and ensure you are getting sufficient restful sleep each night. Create a relaxing bedtime routine and establish a comfortable sleep environment.

> ➢ Nourish your body: Eat a balanced diet that includes nutritious foods to support your overall health. Stay hydrated by drinking an adequate amount of water throughout the day. Pay attention to your body's hunger and fullness cues.

> ➢ Engage in regular exercise: Find physical activities that you enjoy and make them a part of your routine. Exercise not only benefits your physical

health but also releases endorphins that boost your mood and reduce stress.

➢ Practice good hygiene: Take care of your personal grooming, such as bathing, brushing your teeth, and maintaining a clean appearance. These simple self-care practices can contribute to a sense of well-being.

5.3   Emotional and Mental Self-Care

Emotional and mental self-care focuses on nurturing your emotional well-being, managing stress, and maintaining a positive mindset. Consider the following practices:

> Engage in activities that bring you joy: Make time for activities that uplift your spirits and bring you happiness. This can include hobbies, creative outlets, spending time with loved ones, or indulging in activities that make you laugh.

> Practice mindfulness and relaxation techniques: Set aside time for practices such as meditation, deep breathing exercises, or mindfulness activities. These techniques can help you manage stress, increase self-awareness, and promote a sense of calm.

> Seek support when needed: Don't hesitate to reach out for support when you're feeling overwhelmed or struggling with your mental health. Talk to a trusted friend, family member, or mental health professional who can provide guidance and support.

> Engage in self-reflection: Regularly check in with yourself and reflect on your thoughts, feelings, and experiences. Journaling can be a helpful tool for self-reflection and gaining insights into your emotions and patterns of thinking.

5.4   Setting Boundaries and Saying No

Setting boundaries is an essential aspect of self-care. It involves recognizing your limits, communicating your needs, and saying no when necessary. Here's why setting boundaries is important:

> Protects your well-being: Setting boundaries helps prevent burnout and protects your physical and mental health. It allows you to prioritize self-care and allocate time and energy to activities that are meaningful and fulfilling.

> Maintains healthy relationships: Boundaries contribute to healthy and respectful relationships. They establish clear expectations and promote open communication, which leads to stronger connections with others.

> Empowers you: Setting boundaries is an act of self-empowerment. It allows you to assert your needs, make choices that align with your values, and take control of your life.

Practice assertiveness when setting boundaries. Clearly communicate your needs, limits, and expectations. Be firm and respectful, and remember that it is your right to prioritize your well-being.

5.5 Cultivating Self-Compassion

Self-compassion is the practice of treating yourself with kindness, understanding, and acceptance, especially during difficult times. Here's how cultivating self-compassion can contribute to your emotional well-being:

- ➤ Reduces self-criticism: Self-compassion helps counteract self-criticism and the harsh inner dialogue that can contribute to depression. Instead of berating yourself for perceived shortcomings, practice self-compassion by offering yourself understanding and forgiveness.

- ➤ Increases resilience: When faced with challenges or setbacks, self-compassion enables you to respond with resilience and self-care. Rather than dwelling on failures, you can acknowledge your emotions, learn from the experience, and move forward with self-compassion and self-belief.

To cultivate self-compassion, consider the following practices:

- ➤ Practice self-kindness: Treat yourself with the same kindness and compassion you would extend to a loved one. Speak to yourself in a gentle and supportive manner, offering understanding and encouragement.

- ➤ Embrace your imperfections: Recognize that imperfections are a natural part of being human. Embrace your flaws and mistakes as opportunities for growth and learning, rather than sources of self-judgment.

- ➤ Practice mindfulness: Be present with your thoughts and emotions without judgment. Notice and validate your feelings, allowing yourself to experience them fully while maintaining a compassionate attitude toward yourself.

> Seek support: Surround yourself with a supportive network of friends, family, or mental health professionals who can offer guidance and understanding. Share your struggles and allow yourself to receive support without judgment.

5.6 The Importance of Leisure and Pleasure

In the midst of busy lives, it is crucial to prioritize leisure and pleasure as part of your self-care routine. Engaging in enjoyable activities promotes a sense of joy, fulfillment, and overall well-being. Consider the following:

> Identify activities that bring you joy: Take time to discover activities that truly bring you pleasure and make you feel alive. It could be hobbies, creative pursuits, outdoor adventures, or simply spending quality time with loved ones.

> Prioritize leisure time: Schedule regular periods of leisure in your routine, where you can engage in activities purely for enjoyment. Treat these moments as non-negotiable and honor them as you would any other important commitment.

> Practice being present: When engaging in leisure activities, be fully present and savor the experience. Allow yourself to let go of worries and distractions, and immerse yourself in the moment.

➢ Embrace playfulness: Cultivate a sense of playfulness and curiosity in your life. Allow yourself to be spontaneous, explore new interests, and approach tasks with a light-hearted attitude.

NOTE: Cultivating self-compassion is a powerful tool for steering clear of depression and nurturing overall well-being. By practicing self-kindness, shifting to a self-compassionate mindset, embracing forgiveness, and integrating self-compassion into daily life, you can develop a more nurturing and supportive relationship with yourself. Remember that self-compassion is a lifelong practice that requires patience and self-awareness. As you continue to cultivate self-compassion, you will experience greater resilience, inner peace, and a deeper sense of self-acceptance. By prioritizing physical and mental self-care, setting healthy boundaries, cultivating self-compassion, and embracing leisure and pleasure, you can navigate the path towards emotional well-being and reduce the risk of depression.

Chapter 6: Overcoming Obstacles and Resilience

6.1 Understanding Obstacles on the Path to Well-being

In this final chapter we look at understanding How there will always be obstacles to the righteous path. On the path to well-being, it's inevitable to encounter obstacles and challenges. In this chapter, we will explore common obstacles and provide strategies to overcome them, fostering resilience and maintaining your progress.

6.2 Identifying Common Obstacles

Recognizing the obstacles that may arise can better equip you to overcome them. Common obstacles include:

- ❖ Self-doubt and negative self-talk: Negative self-talk can undermine your progress and lead to self-doubt. Recognize these patterns and challenge negative thoughts with positive affirmations and self-compassion.

- ❖ Stress and overwhelm: High levels of stress and overwhelm can hinder your well-being. Implement stress-management techniques, such as time management, prioritization, and self-care practices, to reduce stress levels.

- ❖ Setbacks and failures: Setbacks and failures are a natural part of life. Embrace them as opportunities for growth and learning, and use them as motivation to continue on your path towards well-being.

6.3   Embracing Flexibility and Adaptability

- ❖ Flexibility and adaptability are essential traits when overcoming obstacles. Consider the following strategies:
- ❖ Embrace change: Rather than resisting change, approach it with an open mind and a willingness to adapt. See change as an opportunity for growth and new possibilities.
- ❖ Cultivate problem-solving skills: Develop your problem-solving abilities to tackle challenges effectively. Break problems down into manageable steps and seek creative solutions.
- ❖ Practice mindfulness: Cultivate present-moment awareness and non-judgmental acceptance of your circumstances. Mindfulness allows you to respond to challenges with clarity and resilience.

6.4   Learning from Setbacks and Failures

Setbacks and failures can be valuable learning experiences. Consider the following strategies to learn and grow from these experiences:

- ❖ Reflect on the lessons: Take time to reflect on setbacks and failures, identifying the lessons and insights they provide. Use these lessons to adjust your approach and improve your well-being strategies.

❖ Embrace a growth mindset: Embrace a growth mindset that views setbacks as opportunities for growth and improvement. See failure as a natural part of the learning process and a stepping stone towards success.

❖ Seek support: Reach out to your support network or seek guidance from professionals when facing setbacks or failures. Their perspectives and expertise can provide valuable guidance and support.

6.5 Celebrating Resilience and Progress

Recognize and celebrate your resilience and progress along the journey. Acknowledge the obstacles you have overcome, the lessons you have learned, and the growth you have experienced.

❖ Celebrate milestones: Set milestones along your well-being journey and celebrate when you achieve them. This reinforces your progress and motivates you to continue moving forward.

❖ Practice self-appreciation: Take time to appreciate and acknowledge your resilience and determination. Give yourself credit for the steps you have taken and the progress you have made.

NOTE: Overcoming obstacles and fostering resilience is an integral part of sustaining well-being. By identifying common obstacles, developing resilience, embracing flexibility and adaptability, learning from setbacks and failures, and celebrating your progress, you can navigate challenges with confidence and continue on your path towards a fulfilling and balanced life. Remember, resilience is a skill that can be cultivated and strengthened over time.

In Conclusion

Living a life free from depression requires a holistic approach that addresses various aspects of your well-being. By incorporating the strategies and practices outlined in this book, such as developing emotional resilience, managing stress, nurturing connections, and practicing self-care and self-compassion, you can greatly enhance your ability to steer clear of depression and live a fulfilling and balanced life.

Remember that everyone's journey is unique, and it may take time to find the strategies that work best for you. Be patient and compassionate with yourself as you navigate the ups and downs. Seek support when needed and celebrate even the smallest victories along the way. With dedication, self-awareness, and a commitment to your well-being, you can create a life that is characterized by carefree joy, emotional resilience, and a thriving spirit.

May this guide serve as a compass to help you steer free from depression, empowering you to live a life of fulfillment and emotional well-being.